T0190849

THE OFFICIAL GRAPHIC NOVEL

# SPORTS SUPERHEROES

VOL. #1

# STEPHEN CURRY

To Megan, Zach, and Max . . . you are my superheroes (sorry, it was right there!)—JB

For Ella, Oscar, and Kim—my favorite superheroes, villains, and jokers!—RK

PENGUIN WORKSHOP
An imprint of Penguin Random House LLC, New York

First published in the United States of America by Penguin Workshop, an imprint of Penguin Random House LLC, New York, 2024

Creative Direction by Erick Peyton
Content Editor Kalyna Maria Kutny
Design by Mary Claire Cruz



Visit us online at penguinrandomhouse.com.

Library of Congress Cataloging-in-Publication Data is available.

Printed in the United States of America

ISBN 9780593382462 (pbk) 10 9 8 7 6 5 4 3 2 1 PC
ISBN 9780593382486 (hc) 10 9 8 7 6 5 4 3 2 1 PC

This is a work of nonfiction narrated by fictional characters. The events that unfold in the narrative are rooted in historical fact. Some characters have been created and the dialogue of some historical figures has been fictionalized in service of the narrative.

THE OFFICIAL GRAPHIC NOVEL

# SPORTS SUPERHEROES

VOL. #1

# STEPHEN CURRY

BY JOSH BYCEL AND RICH KORSON

ILLUSTRATED BY DAMION SCOTT

LETTERING BY HASSAN OTSMANE-ELHAOU

Unanimous Publishing

Penguin Workshop

# CHAPTER ONE

# THE SPORTS SUPERHEROES

NEW YORK CITY. MANHATTAN.
SOMETIME IN THE NEAR FUTURE.
(But not that far into the future where the robots run the world. That's a story for another time.)

WELCOME TO THE MOST FAMOUS ARENA IN THE WORLD!
West 33rd St
Eighth Ave
ONE WAY
ONE WAY
NEW YORK STA
MASKED
USED A SOCCE
TO APPREHEND
ARMED FUGITIVES

THESE SEATS ARE *SICK*– I COULD RUN ON THE COURT AND HIT A *THREE!*
WAIT, YOU'RE NOT *REALLY* GONNA DO THAT, RIGHT?
NO, JESSE, I'M JUST GETTING AHEAD OF MYSELF. BUT I STILL CAN'T BELIEVE WE GOT THEM JUST FOR CLEANING UP OUR SCHOOL'S PLAYGROUND!

A FEW DAYS EARLIER...
OH YEAH, IT WAS *RAINING!*

ALLSTARS

## MAYA MOSES

**AGE: 11**

- CAPTAIN OF HER SCHOOL'S BASKETBALL, SOCCER, BASEBALL, AND FLAG FOOTBALL TEAMS.
- FEARLESS, PASSIONATE, OUTSPOKEN, AND VERY CURIOUS. A *BIG* RISK-TAKER.

**HEIGHT: 5'2"**

- FAVORITE FOOD IS BUFFALO CHICKEN WINGS.
- FAVORITE PLAYER IS STEPHEN CURRY.

# JESSE WILLIAMSON

**AGE: 11**

- MANAGER OF HIS SCHOOL'S BASKETBALL, SOCCER, BASEBALL, AND FLAG FOOTBALL TEAMS.
- SUPER SMART, CAUTIOUS, A *"STAT GEEK,"* AND NOT A RISK-TAKER.

**HEIGHT: 4'8"**

- FAVORITE FOOD IS BUTTER PASTA.
- FAVORITE PLAYER IS STEPHEN CURRY.

AND THAT'S THE END OF THE FIRST QUARTER!
BAAAAAAAAAAAAA
SWISH
COME ON, LET'S GO TO THE BATHROOM.
BUT I DON'T HAVE TO PEE.
A FANS GUIDE TO BASKETBALL ANALYTICS
I KNOW, DUDE, I JUST WANT TO EXPLORE WITHOUT THE DADS.
OH, YES, I HAVE TO MAKE A PEE-PEE. RIGHT NOW.

DING!
UNKNOWN NUMBER
See that unmarked door? It's open, go for it!
THAT'S SUPER WEIRD. WHO'S SENDING YOU A TEXT?
UNMARKED DOOR
DING!
Tell Jesse it's not weird. We promis

# CHAPTER TWO

# THIS IS WEIRD!

SEE, I TOLD YOU THIS WAS A BAD IDEA.
IT SMELLS LIKE WINDEX AND FEET IN HERE!
KLIK
AAAAH!!

THAT WAS AWESOME!
COOL SECRET ELEVATOR.
CURRY 30


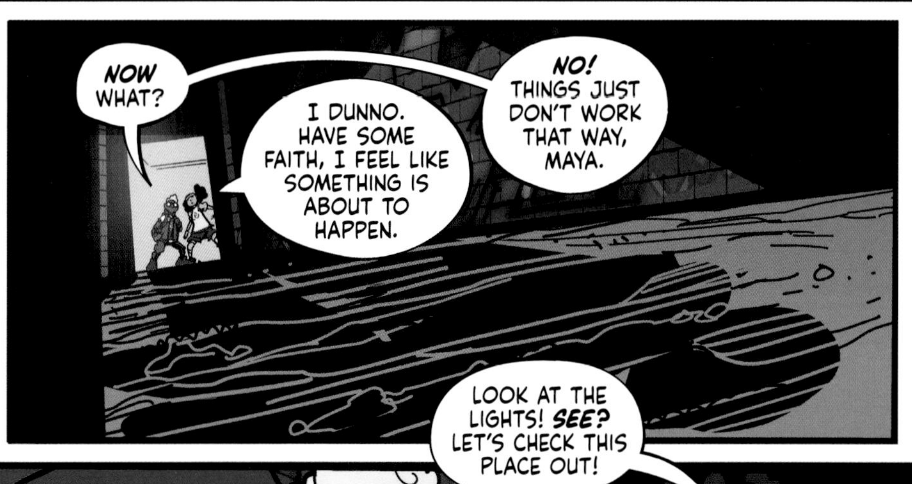

NOW WHAT?
I DUNNO. HAVE SOME FAITH, I FEEL LIKE SOMETHING IS ABOUT TO HAPPEN.
NO! THINGS JUST DON'T WORK THAT WAY, MAYA.


LOOK AT THE LIGHTS! **SEE?** LET'S CHECK THIS PLACE OUT!

*I'M NOT SURE THAT'S THE BEST PLAAAAANNN...*

WHOA!
I KNOW...

WHOA!
I KNOW.

WELCOME TO THE SPORTS SUPERHEROES THRONE ROOM!
WE ARE THE SPORTS SUPERHEROES!

I'M SORRY. THE *WHO NOW?*
IS THIS SOME SORT OF *YOUTUBE PRANK SHOW* THAT COMES WITH OUR TICKETS? IS THERE AN APP I NEED TO DOWNLOAD?

NO, JESSE. IT'S *NOT* A *PRANK SHOW!*

ARE YOU SURE *THESE* ARE THE KIDS WE CHOSE?

WE ARE A SECRET SOCIETY OF ATHLETES, EACH OF US A LEGEND IN OUR OWN SPORT–
–BROUGHT TOGETHER WITH THE GOAL OF PROTECTING THE JOY OF SPORTS, THE LEGACY OF ATHLETICS, AND ALL THAT IS PURE AND GOOD ON THE FIELD OF COMPETITION–
–FROM ALL THE CHEATING, GREED, AND INJUSTICE IN THE WORLD TODAY.

OH, SO YOU'RE LIKE A JUSTICE LEAGUE FOR SPORTS?

?!
WHAT?
NO.
WE'RE WAY COOLER THAN THAT.

SO LIKE THE AVENGERS FOR SPORTS?

SORT OF
NO, NOT THAT EITHER. STOP COMPARING US! WE'RE OUR OWN THING!
A WAY COOLER THING.

OKAY, JEEZ, SORRY.

JESSE AND MAYA, YOU HAVE BEEN CHOSEN, BECAUSE OF YOUR SPECIFIC SKILLS, TO HELP US FIND THE NEXT GENERATION OF SPORTS SUPERHEROES. MAYA, FOR YOUR FEARLESSNESS AND ABILITY ON THE COURT AND THE FIELD.
CURRY
30
AND JESSE, FOR YOUR ENCYCLOPEDIC KNOWLEDGE OF STATISTICS AND EVERY LITTLE DETAIL OF ALL THE MOST FAMOUS ATHLETES' LIVES.
WOW, WHO KNEW BEING A HUGE SPORTS NERD WOULD BE USEFUL?!
WAIT, YOU'RE THE ONES WHO SET UP THAT WHOLE THING AT OUR SCHOOL? DID YOU GET US THESE TICKETS? HAVE YOU BEEN FOLLOWING US?
YEAH. THAT IS KINDA WEIRD.
IT'S NOT WEIRD!
WHAT'S WEIRD, JESSE, IS THAT YOU ONLY EAT BUTTER PASTA AND CHICKEN NUGGETS!
NO WAY. I ALSO EAT PIZZA. AND HOW DO YOU KNOW THAT?
BECAUSE WE ARE SUPERHEROES AND WE KNOW EVERYTHING! AND THIS IS A GREAT HONOR THAT A MILLION KIDS WOULD LOVE TO GET!
OKAY, FINE. HAPPY TO HELP.
BUT ARE WE GONNA MISS ANY OF THE GAME OR ARE OUR DADS GONNA FREAK OUT IF WE DON'T COME BACK?

NOPE. ONCE YOU ENTERED THE THRONE ROOM, ALL TIME AND SPACE WERE FROZEN.
ONCE WE ARE DONE HERE, YOU RETURN AS IF YOU NEVER LEFT.

# CHAPTER THREE

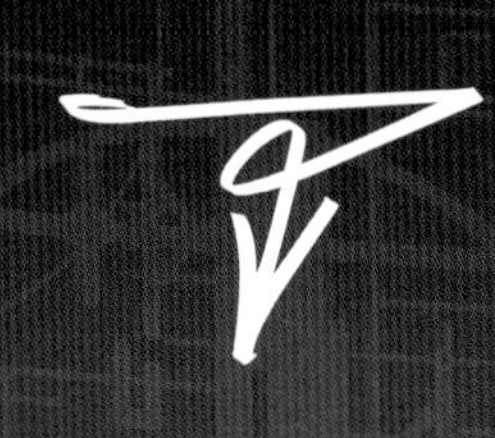

# THE NEXT GENERATION

YEAH, IT'S REALLY FREAKIN' COOL.
SO JUST LIKE THE SPORTS SUPERHEROES BEFORE US, IT IS TIME TO PASS THE TORCH TO A NEW GENERATION. BUT NOT JUST TO ANY ATHLETE— A SPORTS SUPERHERO HAS TO HAVE SO MANY THINGS! LIKE...
PASSION. FAITH. DRIVE.
LOYALTY. SELFLESSNESS. THE WILL TO WIN!
FARTS!
JUST CHECKING TO SEE IF YOU WERE LISTENING.
WAIT, WHAT?

BEING BOLD AND COURAGEOUS!
HAVING A SUPERPOWER!
AND MOST IMPORTANTLY, ALWAYS OVERCOMING ALL THE OBSTACLES IN YOUR WAY!

OKAY, WELL, THAT'S A LOT.

INDEED IT IS. SO, MAYA MOSES AND JESSE WILLIAMSON...
...WHAT CURRENT ATHLETE SHOULD LEAD THIS NEW GENERATION OF SPORTS SUPERHEROES?

STEPHEN CURRY!!!

PULL UP A PICTURE OF STEPHEN CURRY!
WHOA! THAT IS SO COOL.
YEAH, WE HAVE SOME SWEET SUPERHERO STUFF DOWN HERE.
OKAY, DON'T FLEX. THAT'S NOT COOL.

YOU NEED TO UNDERSTAND THAT BEING A GREAT ATHLETE IS ONE THING, BUT BEING A SPORTS SUPERHERO IS SO MUCH MORE. YOU HAVE TO BE A GREAT HUMAN AND YOU NEED TO BE SPECIAL.
IF YOU TRULY BELIEVE STEPHEN CURRY IS WORTHY OF THIS HONOR, THEN YOU NEED TO CONVINCE US. TELL US HIS ORIGIN STORY. EVERY GREAT SUPERHERO ORIGIN STORY IS EITHER FORGED FROM TRAUMA, DESTINY, OR CHANCE.
OR A SPIDER BITE?!
YOU KNOW, 'CAUSE PETER PARKER GOT BIT BY A RADIOACTIVE SPIDER... AND THEN HE BECAME... FORGET IT. CONTINUE...
AS WE WERE SAYING... WHAT IS STEPHEN'S?
OH, THAT'S EASY. STEPHEN'S IS DESTINY. HE WAS BORN TO BE A SUPERHERO.

AKRON, OHIO.
WARDELL STEPHEN CURRY II WAS BORN ON MARCH 14, 1988, IN AKRON, OHIO.
HIS DAD, DELL CURRY, WAS AN NBA PLAYER, AND HIS MOM, SONYA CURRY, WAS AN AMAZING COLLEGE VOLLEYBALL PLAYER...

"...BECAUSE OF HIS SIZE, HE WAS ALWAYS UNDERRATED AND DISRESPECTED.
DAVIDSON 30
"EVERYONE SAID HE WASN'T BIG ENOUGH, STRONG ENOUGH, OR FAST ENOUGH TO MAKE IT.
SMAK
DAVIDSON
"BUT THE GREAT THING ABOUT HIM WAS THAT HE BELIEVED IN HIMSELF. HE ALWAYS HAD FAITH THAT HE WOULD OVERCOME ANY OBSTACLE TO MAKE IT."
"OOH, IS THAT A THEME? THE SPORTS SUPERHEROES LOVE A THEME. CONTINUE."

"WHILE HIS DAD WAS PLAYING FOR NBA TEAMS ALL OVER THE COUNTRY, STEPHEN WAS BACK HOME IN CHARLOTTE. WHEN HE WAS IN EIGHTH GRADE, HIS FAMILY MOVED TO TORONTO.

AND *CANADA* WAS WHERE HE REALLY GOT GOING!

TORONTO. 2000. QUEENSWAY CHRISTIAN COLLEGE.
QUEENSWAY CHRISTIAN COLLEGE
"STEPHEN AND HIS YOUNGER BROTHER, SETH, WERE THE STARS OF THEIR MIDDLE-SCHOOL TEAM. THEY WERE *UNDEFEATED* WHEN THEIR SCHOOL WENT UP AGAINST A *HIGH SCHOOL* TEAM."

"THESE GUYS WERE SICK OF STEPHEN SCORING OVER THEM–
"–SO THEY DECIDED TO GET MEAN AND PHYSICAL AND STARTED PUSHING STEPHEN AROUND!"

HOME: 44
AWAY: 50

:49

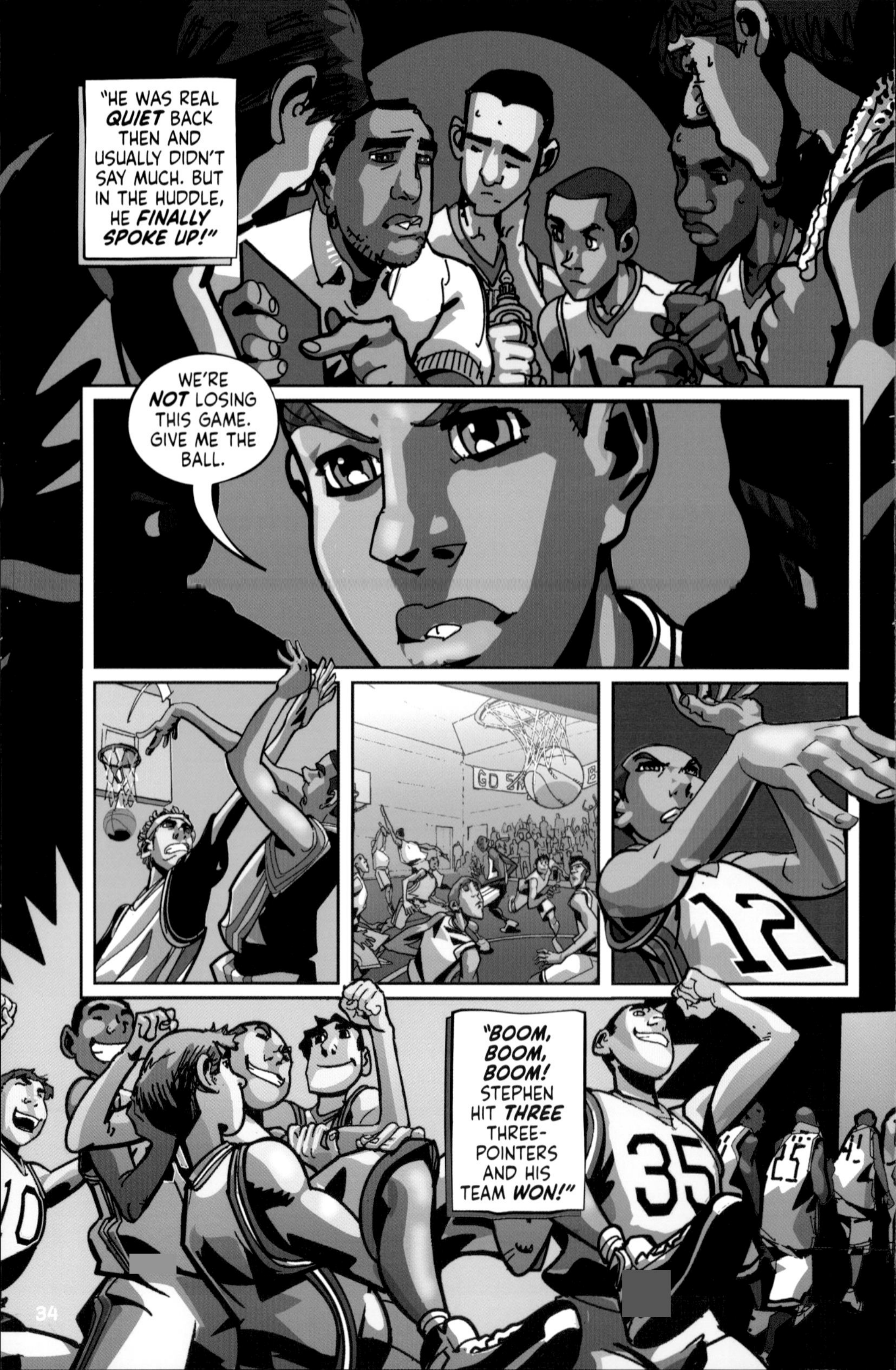
"HE WAS REAL QUIET BACK THEN AND USUALLY DIDN'T SAY MUCH. BUT IN THE HUDDLE, HE FINALLY SPOKE UP!"
WE'RE NOT LOSING THIS GAME. GIVE ME THE BALL.
"BOOM, BOOM, BOOM! STEPHEN HIT THREE THREE-POINTERS AND HIS TEAM WON!"

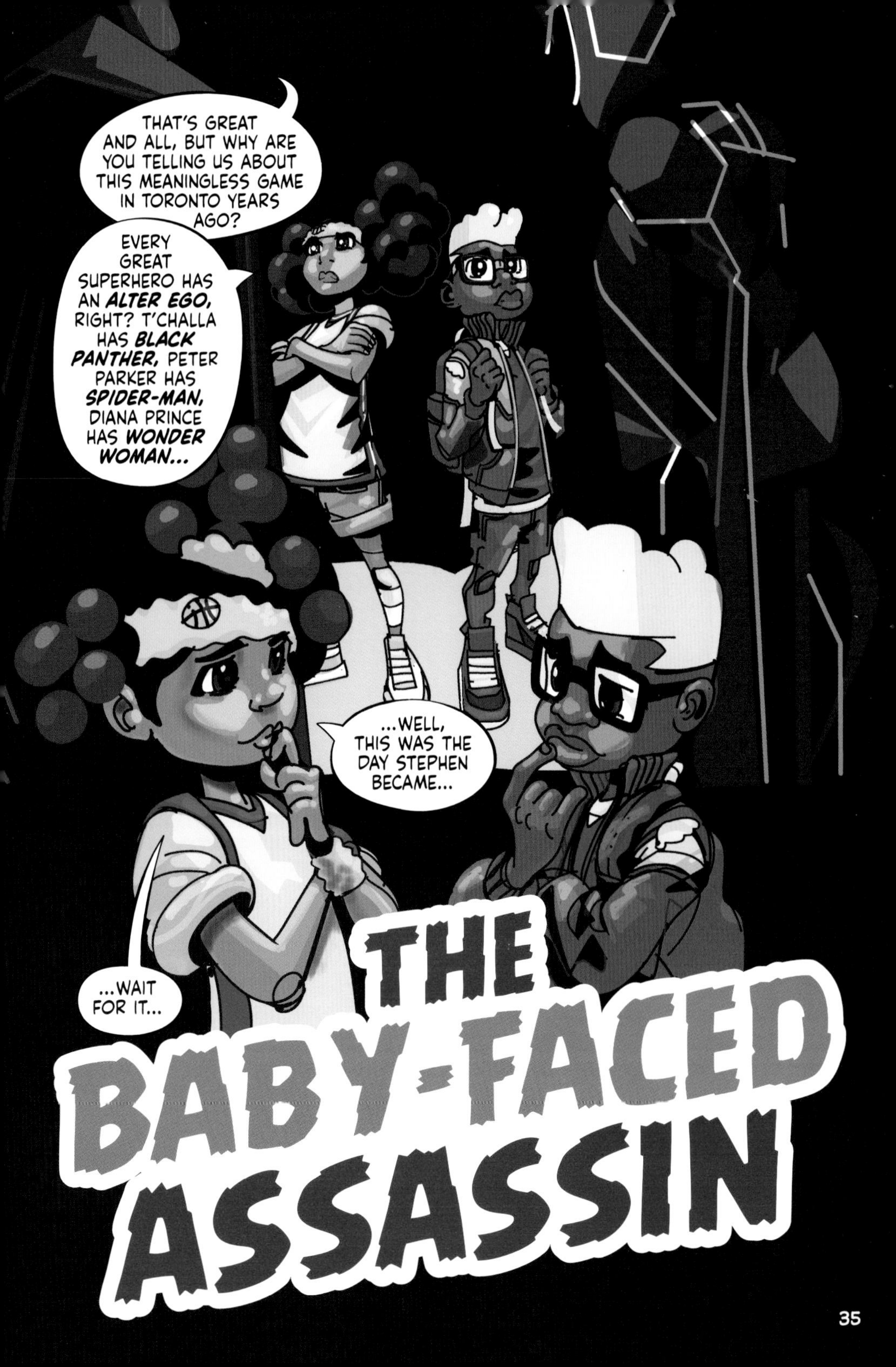
THAT'S GREAT AND ALL, BUT WHY ARE YOU TELLING US ABOUT THIS MEANINGLESS GAME IN TORONTO YEARS AGO?
EVERY GREAT SUPERHERO HAS AN ALTER EGO, RIGHT? T'CHALLA HAS BLACK PANTHER, PETER PARKER HAS SPIDER-MAN, DIANA PRINCE HAS WONDER WOMAN...
...WELL, THIS WAS THE DAY STEPHEN BECAME...
...WAIT FOR IT...
THE BABY-FACED ASSASSIN

THAT IS A GREAT SUPERHERO ALTER EGO.
THAT WILL WORK.

YOU BET YOUR SECRET BUTTS IT WILL.

DID YOU JUST REFER TO OUR SUPERHERO BUTTS?

YEAH. IS THERE A PROBLEM?

UH, NO. NOPE, JUST CHECKING. CARRY ON.
♪♫

ALL-STAR NBA CHAMPION STEPHEN CURRY BECOMES...

# THE BABY-FACED ASSASSIN

"STEPHEN BECOMES THE ***BABY-FACED ASSASSIN*** WHEN PEOPLE DOUBT HIM OR BULLY HIM OR DON'T RESPECT HIM.

"WHEN THE ASSASSIN COMES OUT, FOOLS BETTER WATCH OUT 'CAUSE HE IS ***COMING FOR THEM!"***

# CHAPTER FOUR

# NO ONE GETS TO WRITE YOUR STORY

ONE OF THE BIGGEST MOMENTS IN STEPHEN'S LIFE WAS WHEN HE WAS THIRTEEN YEARS OLD AND HE WAS PLAYING IN A BIG TOURNAMENT— THE AAU NATIONAL CHAMPIONSHIPS—
—AGAINST ALL THE BEST PLAYERS FROM AROUND THE UNITED STATES.
YOU KNOW WHAT? STEPHEN SHOULD REALLY BE TELLING THIS STORY. DOES THAT FANCY BIG SCREEN DO FLASHBACKS?
KID, WE'RE SPORTS SUPERHEROES. OF COURSE IT DOES.
ALL RIGHT THEN, IT WAS THE SUMMER OF 2001 IN TENNESSEE.

SUMMER. 2001. TENNESSEE.
"STEPHEN'S TEAM WAS PLAYING IN A BIG NATIONAL TOURNAMENT.
"BUT THEY LOST BADLY AND HE PLAYED WORSE."
THIS WAS MY CHANCE TO MEASURE MYSELF AGAINST THE BEST PLAYERS AND I FELL SHORT. WAY SHORT. ONLY LESSON I COULD TAKE FROM THIS WAS: I JUST WASN'T GOOD ENOUGH.
THIS WAS ONE OF THE MOST IMPORTANT MOMENTS IN STEPHEN'S LIFE.
STEPHEN SAT DOWN WITH HIS PARENTS IN A SMALL HOTEL ROOM IN TENNESSEE AND THEY LAID IT OUT FOR HIM.
WELL, REALLY IT WAS HIS MOM WHO DID THE TALKING.

MOTEL 5
NO ONE GETS TO WRITE YOUR STORY. NOT SOME SCOUTS OR SOME TOURNAMENT OR EVEN THE KIDS WHO THINK THEY ARE BETTER THAN YOU! NONE OF THESE PEOPLE GET TO BE THE AUTHOR OF ***YOUR*** STORY. JUST ***YOU.***
SO THINK ***REAL HARD*** ABOUT IT. AND THEN YOU GO AND WRITE WHAT YOU WANT TO WRITE. BUT KNOW THAT THIS STORY...
...IT'S ***YOURS.***

# CHAPTER FIVE

# THE SUMMER OF TEARS

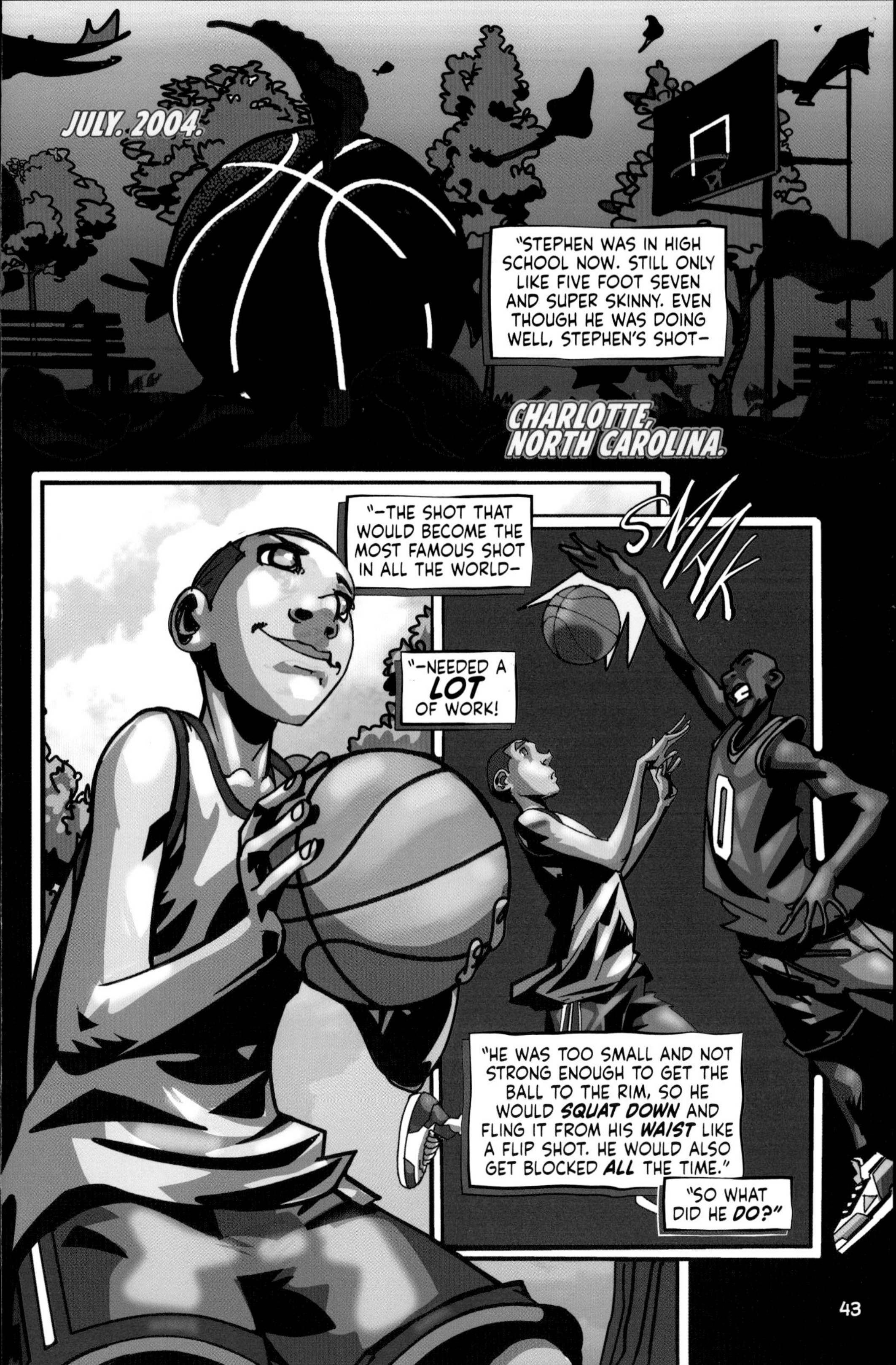
JULY, 2004.
"STEPHEN WAS IN HIGH SCHOOL NOW. STILL ONLY LIKE FIVE FOOT SEVEN AND SUPER SKINNY. EVEN THOUGH HE WAS DOING WELL, STEPHEN'S SHOT–
CHARLOTTE, NORTH CAROLINA.
"–THE SHOT THAT WOULD BECOME THE MOST FAMOUS SHOT IN ALL THE WORLD–
SMAK
"–NEEDED A **LOT** OF WORK!
"HE WAS TOO SMALL AND NOT STRONG ENOUGH TO GET THE BALL TO THE RIM, SO HE WOULD ***SQUAT DOWN*** AND FLING IT FROM HIS ***WAIST*** LIKE A FLIP SHOT. HE WOULD ALSO GET BLOCKED ***ALL*** THE TIME."
"SO WHAT DID HE ***DO?***"

"HE WENT TO WORK.
"HIS DAD KNEW THAT IF STEPHEN EVER WANTED TO PLAY AT THE NEXT LEVEL, HE WOULD HAVE TO **TOTALLY** CHANGE HIS SHOT.
"SO THAT'S WHAT THEY DID.
"ALL. SUMMER. LONG.
"FROM SUNUP TO SUNDOWN THEY WERE IN THE BACKYARD. IN THE **ONE-HUNDRED-DEGREE** NORTH CAROLINA HEAT, NOT SOME **AIR-CONDITIONED GYM.**
"FOR A GUY WHO LOVES TO SHOOT SO MUCH HE SOMETIMES TAKES ONE THOUSAND SHOTS A DAY **BEFORE PRACTICE,** STEPHEN **HATED** IT! HE WAS **MISERABLE.**"
I WANTED TO **QUIT.** I COULDN'T DO **ANYTHING** RIGHT AND NOTHING WAS WORKING. PLUS, **MY ARMS HURT!**

STEPHEN TOOK A LOT OF SHOTS THROUGH MANY TEARS AND SORE MUSCLES. BUT IT WORKED.
HE CHANGED EVERYTHING ABOUT THIS SHOT. HE WAS NOW A SMOOTH, CLEAN, QUICK, EFFICIENT SHOOTING MACHINE.
AND THAT SUMMER ***CHANGED THE COURSE OF NBA HISTORY!***
***WHOA, WHOA.*** OKAY MAYBE WE NEED TO CALM DOWN.
CHANGED THE COURSE OF NBA HISTORY?
***REALLY?***
YEAH, ***REALLY!*** YOU CALL YOURSELVES SPORTS SUPERHEROES, RIGHT? AND EACH ONE OF YOU HAS A ***SUPERPOWER,*** RIGHT?
WELL, STEPHEN'S SUPERPOWER IS HIS
SHOT!
THAT SHOT HAS ***CONQUERED WORLDS, VANQUISHED VILLAINS, BROUGHT PEOPLE SO MUCH JOY,*** AND MADE ***BELIEVERS*** OUT OF ***EVERYONE!***

# CHAPTER SIX

# THE STRAIGHT-UP STATS

YOU KNOW, MY BOY JESSE HERE KNOWS **EVERY** STAT FROM STEPHEN'S CAREER.
YOU WANT HIM TO BREAK IT DOWN FOR YOU?

DO YOU MIND IF I SCREEN SHARE?
SURE.

WHAT'S THE WI-FI PASSWORD?
1111.

**REALLY?** THAT'S PRETTY WEAK, BUT WHATEVER.
HERE WE GO.

FOUR-TIME NBA CHAMPION, TWO-TIME MVP (MOST VALUABLE PLAYER), AND THE SECOND TIME HE BECAME THE ONLY UNANIMOUS CHOICE IN NBA HISTORY.
FINALS MVP, EIGHT-TIME ALL-STAR, TWO-TIME SCORING LEADER, MADE THE MOST THREE-POINTERS IN A SEASON WITH 402, LEADS THE WARRIORS ALL-TIME IN POINTS, ASSISTS, STEALS, AND THREES...
Finals MVP
Eight-Time All-Star
Two-Time Scoring
...OH, AND HE'S WON THREE ESPYS, FOUR BET AWARDS, A TEEN CHOICE AWARD, AND AN OSCAR!

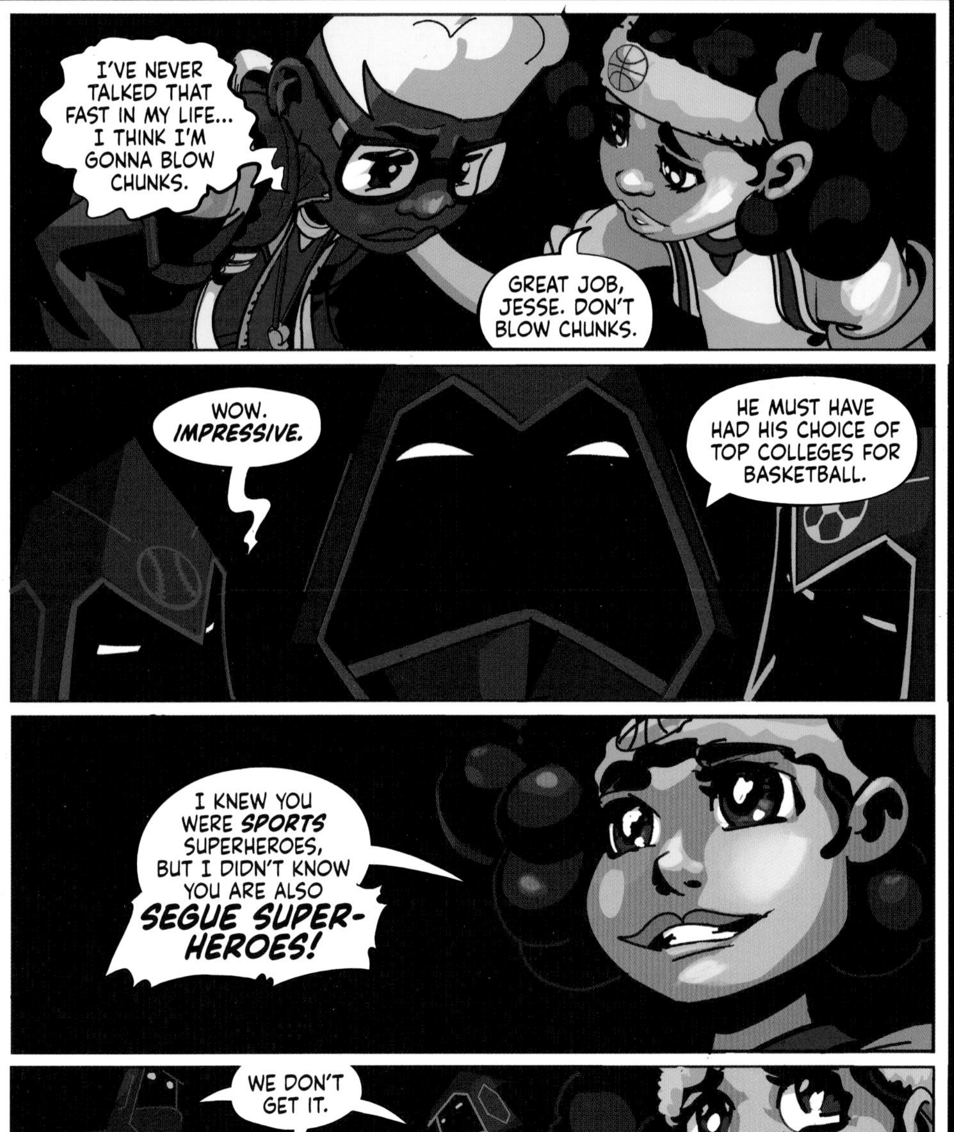
I'VE NEVER TALKED THAT FAST IN MY LIFE... I THINK I'M GONNA BLOW CHUNKS.
GREAT JOB, JESSE. DON'T BLOW CHUNKS.
WOW. IMPRESSIVE.
HE MUST HAVE HAD HIS CHOICE OF TOP COLLEGES FOR BASKETBALL.
I KNEW YOU WERE SPORTS SUPERHEROES, BUT I DIDN'T KNOW YOU ARE ALSO SEGUE SUPER-HEROES!

WE DON'T GET IT.
OKAY, SO SARCASM DOES NOT PENETRATE THE ROBES. GOT IT.
WHAT I'M SAYING IS YOU SET US UP TO TELL YOU ABOUT THE NEXT HURDLE STEPHEN HAD TO OVERCOME. COLLEGE!

EVEN THOUGH HE WAS HIS HIGH-SCHOOL TEAM MVP, HE DIDN'T GET ANY OFFERS FROM THE BIG SCHOOLS.
HE WAS RANKED THE 281ST BEST PLAYER IN THE UNITED STATES HIS SENIOR YEAR. AND THE 51ST BEST POINT GUARD! TALK ABOUT BEING UNDERRATED.
JEEZ!
KNIGHTS
SO, BASICALLY, STEPHEN GOT OFFERS FROM SOME SMALLER SCHOOLS. UNTIL THE DAY VIRGINIA TECH FINALLY CALLED!

# CHAPTER SEVEN

## THE MEETING IN THE CAFETERIA

"SO VIRGINIA TECH IS IN THE ATLANTIC COAST CONFERENCE, THE ACC. IT'S THE HOME OF COLLEGE BASKETBALL BECAUSE MANY CONSIDER IT THE BEST CONFERENCE."
"THIS WAS STEPHEN'S DREAM SCHOOL. IT WAS WHERE BOTH HIS PARENTS HAD BEEN STAR ATHLETES. AND NOW THEY WANTED TO COME TO HIS HIGH SCHOOL AND MEET HIM.
"SO STEPHEN MADE A PLAN."
VIRGI
YOU KNOW WHAT? WE SHOULD REALLY LET STEPHEN TELL THIS STORY.

FALL. 2005. CHARLOTTE CHRISTIAN SCHOOL.
I LEGIT THOUGHT THEY WERE GOING TO MAKE ME AN OFFER. I SUGGESTED WE MEET OVER LUNCH. COOL, RIGHT? VERY PROFESSIONAL.
EXCEPT LUNCH AT MY SCHOOL MEANT IN THE CAFETERIA IN FRONT OF THE ENTIRE STUDENT BODY. ALL 360 OF THEM.
THE VIRGINIA TECH COACH WALKS IN, WEARING A BIG HOKIES SHIRT AND A HOKIES HAT.
VIRGINIA TEC
WE SHAKE HANDS AND SIT DOWN. THE WHOLE SCHOOL IS BUZZING. EVERYONE IS LOOKING AT US! AND I AM STRAIGHT UP FEELING MYSELF RIGHT NOW.
IT'S BASICALLY A POWER LUNCH. I'M ON TOP OF THE WORLD. AND THEN THE DUDE HITS ME WITH...

THANKS FOR MEETING ME. WE'D LIKE TO INVITE YOU...
...TO ***WALK ON.***

WALK ON?!
THOSE ARE THE PLAYERS THAT SIT AT THE END OF THE BENCH AND ALMOST NEVER GET TO PLAY. IT'S STILL COOL, BUT NOT FOR STEPHEN CURRY.
SO HE REMEMBERED WHAT HIS MOM HAD TOLD HIM IN THAT SWEATY HOTEL ROOM IN TENNESSEE.
"WRITE YOUR OWN STORY."

SO THAT'S **EXACTLY** WHAT STEPHEN DID BY COMMITTING TO PLAY FOR **TINY** DAVIDSON COLLEGE. THEY HAD BEEN RECRUITING HIM THE WHOLE TIME.
DAVIDSON 41
DAVIDSON 14
DAVIDSON 2
DAVIDSON 30
DAVIDSON
DAVIDSON 4
DAVIDSON 24
THEIR COACH, BOB McKILLOP, BELIEVED IN HIM. AND FOR STEPHEN, BELIEF WAS SUPER IMPORTANT. JUST LISTEN TO HIM TALK ABOUT HIS EXPERIENCE.
*IT TAUGHT ME PATIENCE. IT TAUGHT ME TO APPRECIATE THE OPPORTUNITY YOU HAVE, AND THAT EVERYTHING HAPPENS FOR A REASON, AND TO EMBRACE WHATEVER YOUR STORY IS.*
*AND THE REST IS* ***HISTORY.***
"AND THAT HISTORY STARTED WITH THE ***2008 NCAA BASKETBALL TOURNAMENT!"***

# CHAPTER EIGHT

# THE WORLD MEETS STEPHEN CURRY

MARCH, 2008.
NCAA (NATIONAL COLLEGE ATHLETIC ASSOCIATION) TOURNAMENT.

# MARCH MADNESS

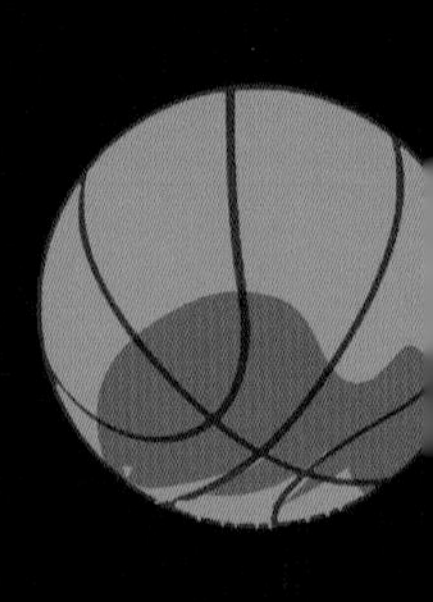

STEPHEN AND HIS TEAM WENT ON A MAGICAL RUN IN THE TOURNAMENT. FIRST THEY BEAT GONZAGA!
"THEN THEY TOOK DOWN NO. 2 GEORGETOWN, AND STEPHEN SCORED 30 POINTS.
30 POINTS
DAVIDSON 30
POINTS
"AND THEN THEY TOOK DOWN THE MIGHTY WISCONSIN BADGERS.
DAVIDSON 30
"STEPHEN SCORED ANOTHER 33, NO BIG DEAL."

STEPHEN AND HIS TEAMMATES HAD BECOME THE DAVIDS BEATING THE GOLIATHS, THE CINDERELLAS OF THE BALL, THE DRAGON SLAYERS SLAYING THE DRAGONS...
ALL RIGHT, JESSE, CALM DOWN.
SORRY. RIGHT. SO THE DREAM ENDED IN THE ELITE EIGHT WITH A LOSS TO KANSAS, WHO WOULD GO ON TO WIN THE WHOLE THING.
DAVIDSON
DAVIDSON
DAVIDSO
STEPHEN AND HIS TEAMMATES' RUN WAS ***LEGENDARY*** AND EVERYONE NOW KNEW THE NAME ***STEPHEN CURRY.*** HE WOULD PLAY ONE MORE YEAR AT DAVIDSON AND THEN DECLARE FOR THE ***NBA DRAFT.***

# CHAPTER NINE

## THE NBA!

STEPHEN HAD BECOME A STAR, BUT ONCE THE NBA DRAFT ROLLED AROUND, IT WAS RIGHT BACK TO BEING DISRESPECTED, UNDERRATED, AND OVERLOOKED. JUST ANOTHER HURDLE FOR MR. CURRY TO OVERCOME.
THIS WAS AN *ACTUAL* SCOUTING REPORT FROM AN NBA TEAM ON STEPHEN.
SPORTS ILLUSTRATED
STEPH CURRY
NOT A TRUE POINT GUARD.
CAREER BACKUP.
AVERAGE ATHLETICISM.
AVERAGE SIZE.
AVERAGE SPEED.
FRAIL FRAME.
VIDSON
SPORTS TODAY
DO NOT RELY ON HIM TO RUN YOUR TEAM!

"JUST LIKE WITH DAVIDSON, SOMEBODY BELIEVED IN STEPHEN. AND THAT SOMEBODY WAS THE GOLDEN STATE WARRIORS.
"HE WAS TAKEN SEVENTH IN THE 2009 NBA DRAFT. AND THE NBA WOULD *NEVER* BE THE *SAME.*"
CURRY 30
BUT NOT YET...

"MONTA ELLIS WAS THE WARRIORS' STAR PLAYER, BUT HE WAS ALSO A GUARD, JUST LIKE STEPHEN.
"THE FIRST DAY STEPHEN JOINED THE TEAM, MONTA SAID THAT THEY COULDN'T PLAY WITH TWO GUYS WHO BASICALLY PLAY THE SAME POSITION."
IT'S NOT GONNA WORK. I WANT TO WIN AND WE ARE NOT GONNA WIN THAT WAY.
"BUT STEPHEN DIDN'T LET IT BOTHER HIM. HE JUST KEPT DOING WHAT HE ALWAYS DID– PROVE EVERYONE WRONG!"

1: Lake
2: Mave
3: Suns
4: Nuggets
5: Jazz
6: Trail Bl
7: Spu
8: Thunde
9:Rockets
10: Grizzlies
11: Hornets
12: Clippers
13: Warriors
14: Kings
15: Timberwolves
BUT THE WARRIORS WERE— I MEAN, LET'S BE HONEST, THEY STUNK! IN STEPHEN'S FIRST TWO SEASONS THEY WON LIKE SIXTY GAMES. TOTAL!
PLUS, STEPHEN'S NEW COACH DIDN'T BELIEVE IN HIM. THE COACH PULLED HIM EVERY TIME HE HAD A TURNOVER OR AT THE END OF A CLOSE GAME. PEOPLE WERE BACK TO SAYING MEAN THINGS ABOUT STEPHEN.
NOT GOOD ENOUGH TO BE AN NBA POINT GUARD!
WILL ONLY EVER BE A JUMP SHOOTER!
AND THEN THE INJURIES STARTED... ALL OF A SUDDEN, STEPHEN WAS BACK TO BEING THAT SAME KID FROM HIGH SCHOOL AND COLLEGE...
...THE KID THAT HAD TO PROVE HIMSELF ALL OVER AGAIN!

# CHAPTER TEN

# THE ANKLES!

DECEMBER 8, 2010.
SAN ANTONIO, TEXAS.
"STEPHEN HAD NEVER REALLY BEEN HURT BEFORE, BUT ON THIS NIGHT HE ROLLED HIS RIGHT ANKLE. WITH NO ONE AROUND HIM!"
"IT DIDN'T SEEM LIKE A BIG DEAL, BUT OVER THE NEXT YEAR HE KEPT HURTING THE SAME ANKLE.
CURRY
30
"OVER AND OVER AGAIN."

BUT EVEN THOUGH THIS WAS A TOUGH TIME FOR STEPHEN, TWO AMAZING THINGS DID HAPPEN IN 2011.
OR SHOULD I SAY, TWO AMAZING *PEOPLE.*

I THINK YOU *SHOULD* SAY TWO AMAZING PEOPLE IF THAT'S WHAT YOU WANT TO SAY.

WOW, YOU SUPERHEROES REALLY *DON'T* GET, LIKE, *ANY* KIND OF COMEDY.

# CHAPTER ELEVEN

## AYESHA AND STEPHEN!

"WE CAN'T TELL YOU THE STORY OF STEPHEN WITHOUT TALKING ABOUT HIS AMAZING WIFE, *AYESHA.*
"THEY MET WHEN THEY WERE TEENAGERS AT CHURCH IN CHARLOTTE, NORTH CAROLINA. BUT AT FIRST THEY WERE BOTH TOO SHY TO TALK TO EACH OTHER."
Ayesha Curry
STEPHEN WAS THE CUTE BOY AT CHURCH THAT ALL THE GIRLS WERE OBSESSED WITH. SO I DECIDED HE WASN'T FOR ME.

THEY FINALLY RECONNECTED WHEN STEPHEN WAS IN LOS ANGELES TO GO TO THE ESPYS IN 2008.
AYESHA WAS LIVING IN LA AT THE TIME. STEPHEN WAS SUPPOSED TO GO TO SOME FANCY HOLLYWOOD PARTY, BUT HE BLEW IT OFF TO HANG WITH HER.

I WASN'T INTERESTED IN DATING ATHLETES BECAUSE I THOUGHT THEY WERE ALL ARROGANT. BUT STEPHEN WAS DIFFERENT. HE WAS ACTUALLY KINDA *GOOFY!*
SHE DIDN'T CARE ABOUT BASKETBALL OR THE NBA OR ANY OF THAT. SHE DIDN'T JUST LET ME DO WHATEVER I WANTED, AND I LIKED THAT.
"AND FROM THEN ON, THEY WERE A COUPLE. EVEN WHEN STEPHEN MADE IT TO THE NBA AND THEY WERE APART, THEY MADE SURE TO *ALWAYS* TALK TO EACH OTHER."

JULY 30, 2011. CHARLOTTE, NORTH CAROLINA.
AND THEN THEY ENDED UP GETTING MARRIED IN THE SAME CHURCH WHERE THEY MET AS TEENAGERS!
"AND NOW THEY HAVE THREE KIDS! PLUS, AYESHA IS AN AMAZING ACTRESS, AUTHOR, AND SUPER-TALENTED CHEF!"
"SO NOW STEPHEN HAD HIS PARTNER IN LIFE, BUT WHAT HE ALSO NEEDED WAS A PARTNER ON THE COURT."

# CHAPTER TWELVE

# THE PROMISED LAND

"2011 WAS ALSO THE YEAR THE WARRIORS DRAFTED KLAY THOMPSON!
"LIKE EVERY GREAT SUPER-HERO, STEPHEN NEEDED HIS RUNNING MATE. MOST PEOPLE THINK THEY ARE THE BEST SHOOTING BACKCOURT IN THE HISTORY OF THE NBA!
"THEY EVEN HAD THE COOLEST NICKNAME EVER— THE SPLASH BROTHERS!"
BROS

Finals
KICK
"THE 2014-2015 SEASON WAS WHEN IT ALL CAME TOGETHER FOR STEPHEN AND HIS TEAM."
"THEY GOT A NEW COACH IN STEVE KERR. HE GAVE STEPHEN THE GREEN LIGHT TO SHOOT WHEREVER HE WANTED."
67 WINS
"KERR ALSO MADE KLAY THOMPSON AND DRAYMOND GREEN PART OF THE CORE THREE, WHO WOULD LEAD THE WARRIORS TO 67 WINS— THE MOST THEY'D EVER WON IN A SEASON!"

"THE SEASON WAS MAGICAL FOR STEPHEN AND HIS TEAM. HE WON HIS FIRST MVP AWARD AND HIS SPEECH WAS *SO* AWESOME."
Finals CHAMPIONS
I FOUND OUT, I ... IN THE CHAIR IN THE CORNER AND
ABOUT THE ... ABOUT ALL THE PEOPLE
HAVE ... EVERY LITTLE PART OF THE STORY
THAT ... LIFE. THERE ARE OBVIOUSLY GOOD
TO SHUT IT DOWN, AND
ALL ... HARD WORK THAT YOU PUT
ME REALIZE HOW BLESSED
ON THIS
ROSS THE
TO BE

JUNE 16, 2015.
CLEVELAND, OHIO.
"THE WARRIORS ROLLED THROUGH THE PLAYOFFS AND BEAT THE CLEVELAND CAVALIERS IN THE FINALS IN SIX GAMES.
"STEPHEN AVERAGED 26 POINTS A GAME.
"HE HAD DONE IT. STEPHEN HAD WON THE MVP AWARD AND A CHAMPIONSHIP. THIS SHOULDA PUT ALL THE HATERS TO REST FOREVER!"
"BUT IT DIDN'T. STEPHEN STILL HAD MANY MORE THINGS TO OVERCOME AND PEOPLE TO PROVE WRONG."
"ALTHOUGH IT DIDN'T SEEM THAT WAY AT FIRST, 'CAUSE THE NEXT YEAR WAS WILD!"

OKAY, SO IF YOU THOUGHT THE 2014–2015 SEASON WAS GOOD, STEPHEN WENT ABSOLUTELY BONKERS IN 2015–2016.
2015–2016
STEPHEN CURRY
30 Points Per Game
402 3-Pointers
GOLDEN STATE WARRIORS
24 Straight Wins
73 Wins–9 Losses
HE AVERAGED MORE THAN 30 POINTS A GAME, HE BROKE HIS OWN RECORD FOR THREE-POINTERS IN A SEASON, AND THE TEAM STARTED 24–0 ON THEIR WAY TO BREAKING THE NBA RECORD OF 73 WINS!
"STEPHEN WON THE MVP AWARD AGAIN, BACK-TO-BACK, AND THIS TIME HE WAS THE ONLY PLAYER EVER IN HISTORY TO BE A UNANIMOUS CHOICE. WHICH MEANS EVERYONE VOTED FOR HIM!"
"EVERYTHING WAS TOTALLY LINED UP FOR STEPHEN AND THE WARRIORS TO WIN ANOTHER CHAMPIONSHIP. BUT LIKE WITH EVERYTHING ELSE IN STEPHEN'S LIFE, IT WOULDN'T BE THAT EASY."

THE 2016 PLAYOFFS WERE SUPPOSED TO BE THE ENDING TO THE MOST AMAZING SEASON **EVER.** BUT RIGHT AWAY THINGS GOT **WEIRD.** STEPHEN HURT HIS ANKLES AGAIN IN THE FIRST GAME OF THE PLAYOFFS. THEN HE CAME BACK AND HURT HIS KNEE AND WAS OUT FOR **TWO WEEKS.**
"BUT THEY **STILL** MADE IT TO THE NBA FINALS. THEY WERE UP THREE GAMES TO ONE ON THE CLEVELAND CAVALIERS. NO TEAM HAD **EVER** COME BACK FROM 3-1 DOWN IN THE NBA FINALS.
CURRY 30
"THE WARRIORS' WIN WAS BASICALLY A **DONE DEAL.**"
"AND THEN IT **WASN'T.**"

"IN A FLASH, THE CAVS WON THREE STRAIGHT GAMES, INCLUDING GAME 7 ON THE WARRIORS' HOME COURT.
"THE GREATEST SEASON IN NBA HISTORY WAS OVER."

# CHAPTER THIRTEEN

# SUPERFRIENDS

NOT GONNA LIE, THE 2016 FINALS WERE PRETTY HARD FOR STEPHEN, HIS TEAMMATES, AND HIS FAMILY.
I **STILL** HAVEN'T GOTTEN OVER GAME 7. THAT'S SOMETHING THAT WILL STAY WITH ME PRETTY MUCH FOREVER. OBVIOUSLY, YOU HATED THE FEELING, BUT IT'S ALSO A **MOTIVATOR** TO COME BACK **EVEN STRONGER** AND TRY NOT TO HAVE THAT FEELING AGAIN.

BUT STEPHEN IS A CHAMPION AND MORE THAN JUST AN ATHLETE- WE THINK HE IS A SPORTS SUPERHERO.
STEPHEN PULLED THE MOST SUPERHERO MOVE EVER. HE CREATED A SUPERTEAM.
OKAY, SO YOU KNOW HOW MARVEL HAS THE AVENGERS, RIGHT? AND DC HAS THE JUSTICE LEAGUE. WELL, STEPHEN AND THE WARRIORS DECIDED IT WAS TIME FOR THEM TO DO THE SAME.
"ENTER KEVIN DURANT! NBA MVP, ONE OF THE BEST PLAYERS EVER!"
"STEPHEN KNEW THAT IF KEVIN JOINED THE TEAM, THEY WOULD BE BETTER THAN EVER. EVEN IF IT MEANT STEPHEN MIGHT HAVE TO SHOOT LESS. HE DIDN'T CARE, HE JUST WANTED TO WIN!"
35
35

The Death Lineup
SO EVERY SUPERHERO CREW NEEDS A NICKNAME RIGHT? WELL, IT WAS TIME FOR THE WORLD TO MEET ***THE DEATH LINEUP!***
STEVE KERR VS THE GOAT
"IT WAS ***STEPHEN CURRY*** AT POINT GUARD. ***KLAY THOMPSON*** AT SHOOTING GUARD. ***ANDRE IGUODALA*** AT SMALL FORWARD.
"***KEVIN DURANT*** AT POWER FORWARD AND ***DRAYMOND GREEN*** AS THE CENTER, EVEN THOUGH HE WAS ONLY LIKE SIX FOOT SIX AND MOST CENTERS ARE WAY, ***WAY*** TALLER!"

WITH STEPHEN AND THE DEATH LINEUP LEADING THE WAY, THE WARRIORS **CRUSHED** EVERY TEAM THEY PLAYED AND WON **BACK-TO-BACK NBA CHAMPIONSHIPS!**
2017.
2018.

STEPHEN AND THE DEATH LINEUP WOULD RUN IT BACK ONE MORE YEAR IN 2019 AND HELP THE WARRIORS MAKE THE FINALS FOR THE *FIFTH STRAIGHT TIME!*
BUT KEVIN DURANT GOT HURT AND THEN KLAY THOMPSON GOT HURT...
"AND THE WARRIORS *LOST* TO THE TORONTO RAPTORS IN THE NBA FINALS, EVEN THOUGH STEPHEN CURRY SCORED *47 POINTS* IN ONE OF THE GAMES."

AFTER THAT, KEVIN DURANT LEFT THE TEAM, KLAY THOMPSON WAS OUT FOR THE SEASON, AND STEPHEN WAS BACK TO BEING IN A PLACE HE KNEW REALLY WELL... THE UNDERDOG.
GREAT JOB, KIDS. WHAT AN AMAZING CAREER STEPHEN CURRY HAS HAD. YOU'VE GIVEN US LOTS TO THINK ABOUT...
WHOA, WHOA, WHOA, OLD SUPERHEROES, WE ARE NOT EVEN CLOSE TO BEING DONE!
YOU KNOW WHAT? OUR COLLECTIVE BAD. PLEASE CONTINUE...
YEAH, EVERY GREAT SUPERHERO ORIGIN STORY HAS THE RISE AND FALL AND THE RISE AGAIN. LIKE IRON MAN. WE AREN'T EVEN TO THE BEST PART YET!
THANK YOU.

# CHAPTER FOURTEEN

# THE LOST YEARS AND BACK TO THE MOUNTAINTOP

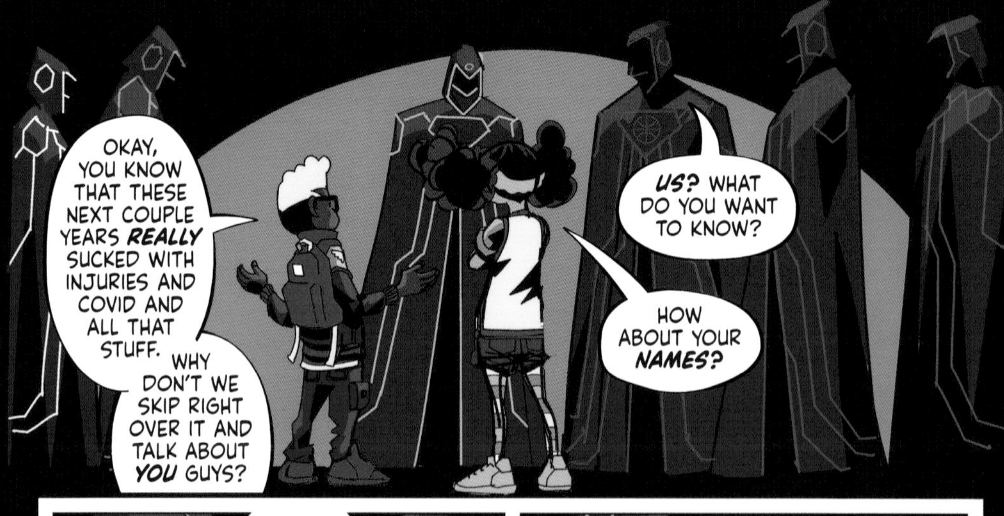
OKAY, YOU KNOW THAT THESE NEXT COUPLE YEARS REALLY SUCKED WITH INJURIES AND COVID AND ALL THAT STUFF.
WHY DON'T WE SKIP RIGHT OVER IT AND TALK ABOUT YOU GUYS?
US? WHAT DO YOU WANT TO KNOW?
HOW ABOUT YOUR NAMES?

OH, WELL, I'M—
SHHHH.
WHAT'RE YOU DOING? YOU CAN'T REVEAL WHO WE ARE? NOT YET, AT LEAST.
OH, RIGHT.
SHE TRICKED ME. YOU ARE TOO SMART, YOUNG LADY, AND I DON'T LIKE IT!
WE ALMOST HAD THEM!

YOU DIDN'T "ALMOST HAVE ME."
LET'S GET BACK TO THE STORY!

"SO, JUST LIKE ALL THE BEST SUPERHERO STORIES, THERE IS THE RISE, AND THE FALL, AND THEN THE ***RISE AGAIN!*** AND THIS IS A GREAT PLACE TO ***START THE RISE,*** BABY!"

"*OH,* DUDE, I ***LOVE*** HOW THIS IS, LIKE, ***TOTALLY*** COMING ***FULL CIRCLE.*** RIGHT UPSTAIRS IS WHERE STEPHEN MADE HISTORY! ***OF COURSE*** HE DID IT ***HERE!***"

"ON THE ***BIGGEST STAGE,*** IN THE ***MOST FAMOUS ARENA IN THE WORLD,*** STEPHEN, ONCE AGAIN, PROVED HE'S THE ***GREATEST SHOOTER OF ALL TIME.***"

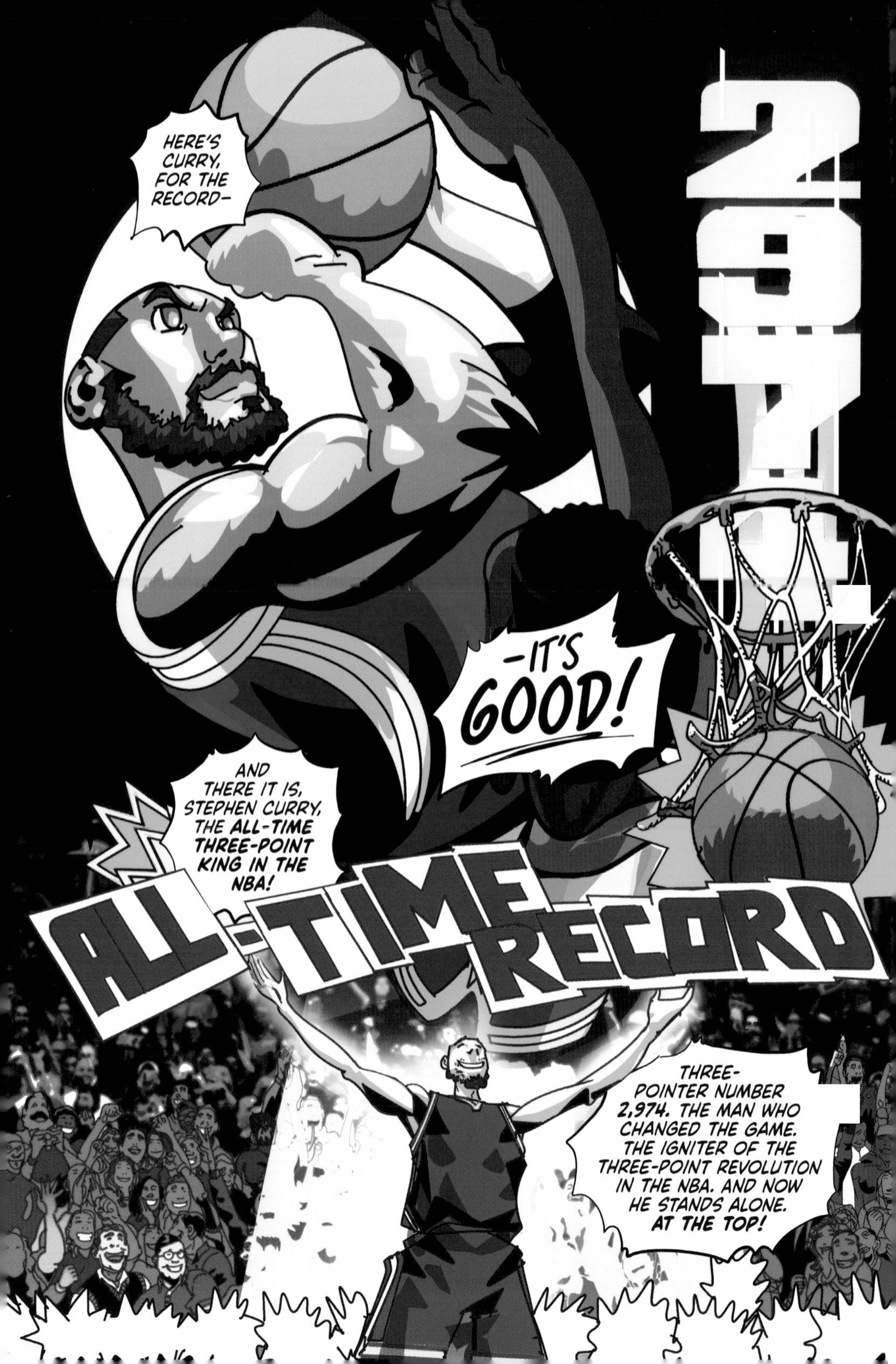
HERE'S CURRY, FOR THE RECORD–
–IT'S GOOD!
AND THERE IT IS, STEPHEN CURRY, THE **ALL-TIME THREE-POINT KING IN THE NBA!**
ALL-TIME RECORD
THREE-POINTER NUMBER 2,974. THE MAN WHO CHANGED THE GAME. THE IGNITER OF THE THREE-POINT REVOLUTION IN THE NBA. AND NOW HE STANDS ALONE. **AT THE TOP!**

I'VE BEEN THINKING ABOUT THIS NUMBER FOR A LONG TIME. I EVEN GOT IT ON MY SHOES.
THAT'S BASKETBALL HISTORY.
CURRY 2974
THE WARRIORS WERE BACK TO WINNING GAMES AND HAVING FUN. STEPHEN SCORED 50 POINTS AT THE NBA ALL-STAR GAME AND WAS NAMED ITS MVP.
THEN ON HIS THIRTY-FOURTH BIRTHDAY, HE SCORED 47 POINTS! AND THEN CAME THE NBA FINALS...

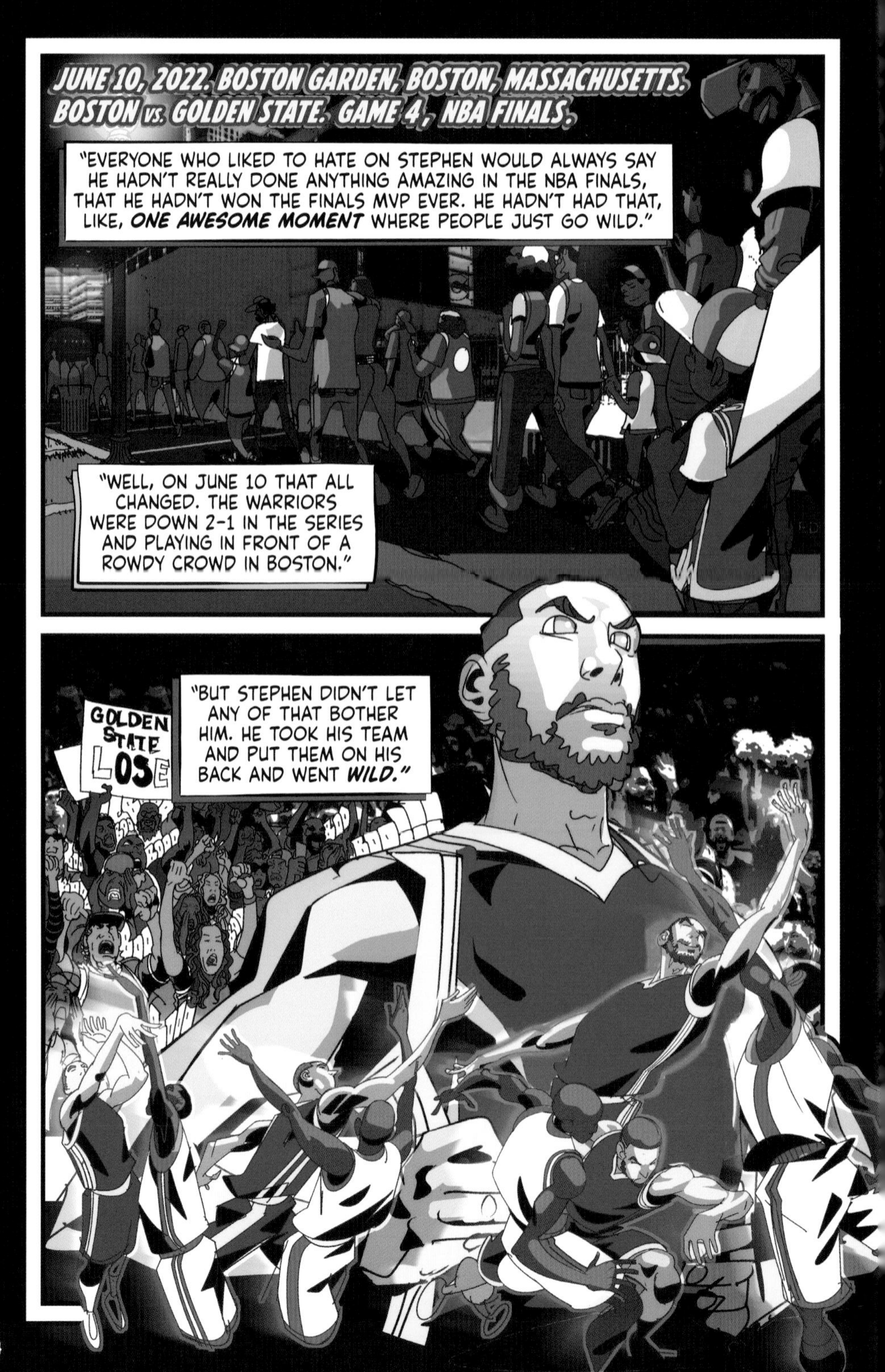
JUNE 10, 2022. BOSTON GARDEN, BOSTON, MASSACHUSETTS.
BOSTON vs. GOLDEN STATE. GAME 4, NBA FINALS.
"EVERYONE WHO LIKED TO HATE ON STEPHEN WOULD ALWAYS SAY HE HADN'T REALLY DONE ANYTHING AMAZING IN THE NBA FINALS, THAT HE HADN'T WON THE FINALS MVP EVER. HE HADN'T HAD THAT, LIKE, ONE AWESOME MOMENT WHERE PEOPLE JUST GO WILD."
"WELL, ON JUNE 10 THAT ALL CHANGED. THE WARRIORS WERE DOWN 2-1 IN THE SERIES AND PLAYING IN FRONT OF A ROWDY CROWD IN BOSTON."
GOLDEN STATE LOSE
"BUT STEPHEN DIDN'T LET ANY OF THAT BOTHER HIM. HE TOOK HIS TEAM AND PUT THEM ON HIS BACK AND WENT WILD."

JUNE 16, 2022.
GAME 6, NBA FINALS.
AND HE WON THE ONE THING THAT HE HAD NEVER GOTTEN: THE NBA FINALS MVP AWARD.
Finals CHAMPIONS
Finals CHAMPIO

# CHAPTER FIFTEEN

## DECISION TIME

SO, ANY QUESTIONS?
NO. I THINK WE'VE HEARD ENOUGH.
NOW THE LAST TEST FOR STEPHEN IS THE THREE PILLARS! WE HAVE THREE PILLARS, THREE WORDS ALL THE SPORTS SUPER-HEROES LIVE BY. A MOTTO OR CREED, IF YOU WILL, AND IT'S...

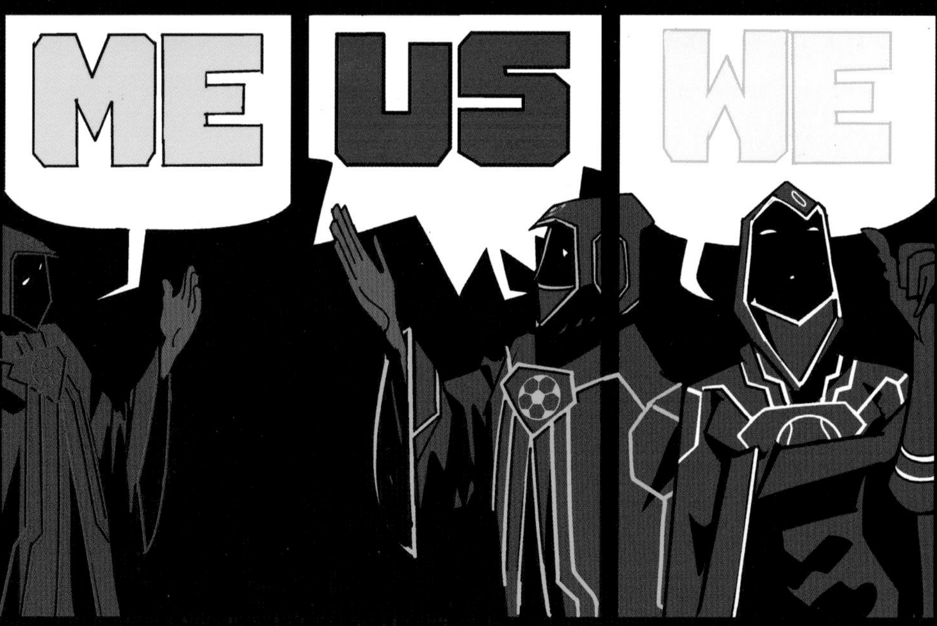
ME
US
WE

COOL. WHAT DOES IT MEAN?

IT MEANS THE FOLLOWING: ME IS THAT YOU HAVE TO WORK THE HARDEST, PUT IN THE MOST TIME, AND BE THE BEST ATHLETE YOU CAN BE.
ME
Pffft.
THAT'S EASY. WE'VE ALREADY TOLD YOU HE'S THE BEST SHOOTER OF ALL TIME. ALSO, HE LITERALLY CHANGED THE WAY PEOPLE PLAY BASKET-BALL.
HE'S A CHEAT CODE. HE UNLOCKED A DIFFERENT STYLE OF BASKETBALL. AND ANYWHERE YOU GO IN THE WORLD, AT ANY AGE, ON ANY COURT, YOU WILL SEE PEOPLE TRYING TO SHOOT LIKE STEPHEN.

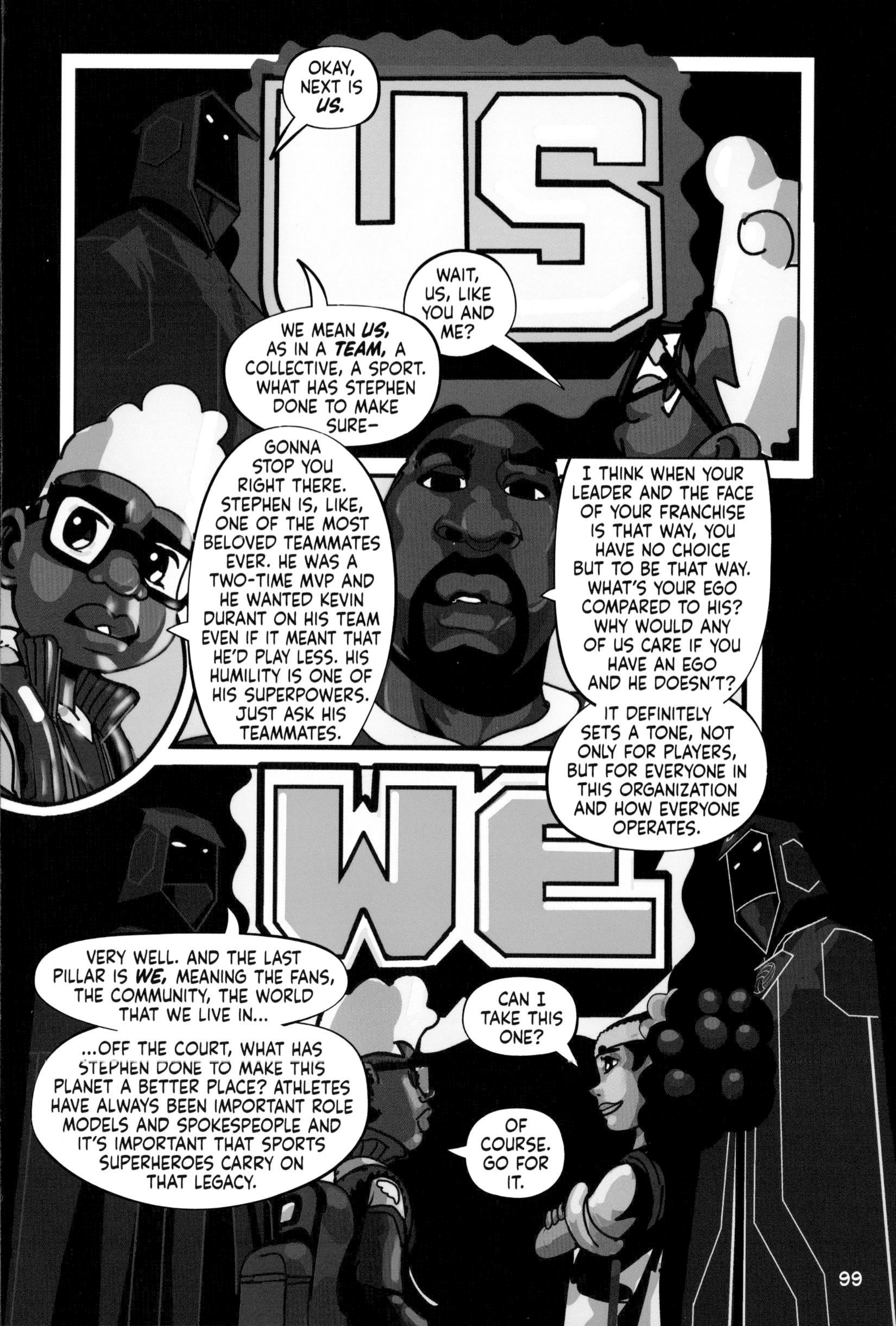
OKAY, NEXT IS US.
US
WAIT, US, LIKE YOU AND ME?
WE MEAN US, AS IN A TEAM, A COLLECTIVE, A SPORT. WHAT HAS STEPHEN DONE TO MAKE SURE—
GONNA STOP YOU RIGHT THERE. STEPHEN IS, LIKE, ONE OF THE MOST BELOVED TEAMMATES EVER. HE WAS A TWO-TIME MVP AND HE WANTED KEVIN DURANT ON HIS TEAM EVEN IF IT MEANT THAT HE'D PLAY LESS. HIS HUMILITY IS ONE OF HIS SUPERPOWERS. JUST ASK HIS TEAMMATES.
I THINK WHEN YOUR LEADER AND THE FACE OF YOUR FRANCHISE IS THAT WAY, YOU HAVE NO CHOICE BUT TO BE THAT WAY. WHAT'S YOUR EGO COMPARED TO HIS? WHY WOULD ANY OF US CARE IF YOU HAVE AN EGO AND HE DOESN'T?
IT DEFINITELY SETS A TONE, NOT ONLY FOR PLAYERS, BUT FOR EVERYONE IN THIS ORGANIZATION AND HOW EVERYONE OPERATES.
WE
VERY WELL. AND THE LAST PILLAR IS WE, MEANING THE FANS, THE COMMUNITY, THE WORLD THAT WE LIVE IN...
...OFF THE COURT, WHAT HAS STEPHEN DONE TO MAKE THIS PLANET A BETTER PLACE? ATHLETES HAVE ALWAYS BEEN IMPORTANT ROLE MODELS AND SPOKESPEOPLE AND IT'S IMPORTANT THAT SPORTS SUPERHEROES CARRY ON THAT LEGACY.
CAN I TAKE THIS ONE?
OF COURSE. GO FOR IT.

EAT. LEARN. PLAY
STEPHEN HAS SPENT HIS LIFE DOING THE RIGHT THINGS. AND HE ESPECIALLY WANTS TO HELP IN HIS ADOPTED HOMETOWN OF OAKLAND. HE AND AYESHA STARTED THIS ORGANIZATION CALLED THE ***EAT. LEARN. PLAY. FOUNDATION...*** IT'S ***SO*** COOL.
***"EAT"*** IS THE FIRST PART. THEY DELIVER FOOD AND MEALS TO KIDS IN NEED IN OAKLAND, CALIFORNIA, AND AROUND THE COUNTRY!
AS AYESHA SAYS...
EVERY MISSED MEAL COUNTS FOR A KID, BECAUSE AN EMPTY STOMACH THAT HURTS TODAY ALSO HURTS THEIR FUTURES.
"AND THEN THE ***'LEARN'*** PART IS ALSO COOL. THEY ARE BUILDING LITTLE TOWN LIBRARIES IN HUNDREDS OF SCHOOLS IN OAKLAND, SO KIDS WHO DON'T NORMALLY HAVE ACCESS TO BOOKS CAN LEARN TO LOVE TO READ.

"AND THEN ***'PLAY'*** IS, OF COURSE, MY FAVORITE. STEPHEN AND AYESHA ARE REBUILDING PLAYGROUNDS AND CREATING NEW SPACES FOR KIDS WHO DON'T HAVE ANYWHERE TO PLAY. I'D SAY THAT'S PRETTY COOL."

I THINK WE HAVE ENOUGH TO MAKE A DECISION.
YA THINK? WE'VE BEEN TALKING FOR HOURS. IT'S A NO-BRAINER.
I THINK NOW WE CAN LET YOU IN ON A COUPLE LITTLE SECRETS.
A: THESE ROBES ARE SUPER ITCHY!
AND B: WE ALREADY KNEW A LOT OF THIS STUFF ABOUT STEPHEN'S LIFE.

WHAT?!
THEN WHY DID WE HAVE TO GO THROUGH ALL THAT?

BECAUSE WE NEEDED TO SEE STEPHEN THROUGH YOUR EYES. KIDS' EYES. BECAUSE YOUR LOVE OF ATHLETES AND SPORTS IS STILL PURE. WHAT WE DO HERE IS MORE IMPORTANT NOW THAN IT'S EVER BEEN. WITH ALL THE MONEY AND CHEATING AND INABILITY FOR PEOPLE TO EVEN HAVE ACCESS TO BEING AN ATHLETE...
...THE JOY OF SPORTS IS IN DANGER OF BEING LOST FOREVER. THAT IS WHY WE NEED YOU TO HELP US FIND A NEW GENERATION OF SPORTS SUPERHEROES.
THAT IS SO SWEET. NOW CAN WE VOTE?!

ALL IN FAVOR OF MAKING WARDELL STEPHEN CURRY II THE FIRST MEMBER OF THE NEXT GENERATION OF SPORTS SUPERHEROES...
CAN WE CHANGE THAT TO SPORTS SUPERHEROES 2.0? NO? IT'S COOL, WE CAN WORKSHOP THAT LATER.

BOOM BOOM BOOM
BOOM BOOM BOOM

WHAT'S HAPPENING? WHAT AM I DOING HERE?

OH MY GOD, IT'S STEPHEN CURRY!
OKAY, LEMME EXPLAIN REAL FAST–
–THESE OLD PEEPS IN THE ROBES ARE THE SPORTS SUPERHEROES, LEGENDS AND FAMOUS ATHLETES. THEY WERE FORMED A SUPER LONG TIME AGO WITH THE GOAL OF PROTECTING SPORTS AND ATHLETES AND UNDERDOGS AND OTHER STUFF I CAN'T TOTALLY REMEMBER...

KINDA LIKE THE AVENGERS FOR SPORTS.
WE HEARD THAT!

THESE CHILDREN HAVE NOMINATED *YOU* TO LEAD THE NEXT GENERATION OF SPORTS SUPERHEROES IN OUR FIGHT...
CURRY
30
YOU DID THAT FOR *ME?*
IT WAS NOTHING.

WARDELL STEPHEN CURRY II, WILL YOU JOIN THE SPORTS SUPERHEROES IN OUR QUEST TO PROTECT THE JOY OF SPORTS, THE LEGACY OF ATHLETICS, AND ALL THAT IS PURE AND GOOD ON THE FIELD OF COMPETITION?
IF SO, ARE YOU READY TO JOIN THE STARTING LINEUP OF THE SPORTS SUPERHEROES?
OH, I LIKE HOW YOU BROUGHT IT FULL CIRCLE WITH A SPORTS METAPHOR.
I AM.

WELL, THIS IS AWESOME.

WARRIORS

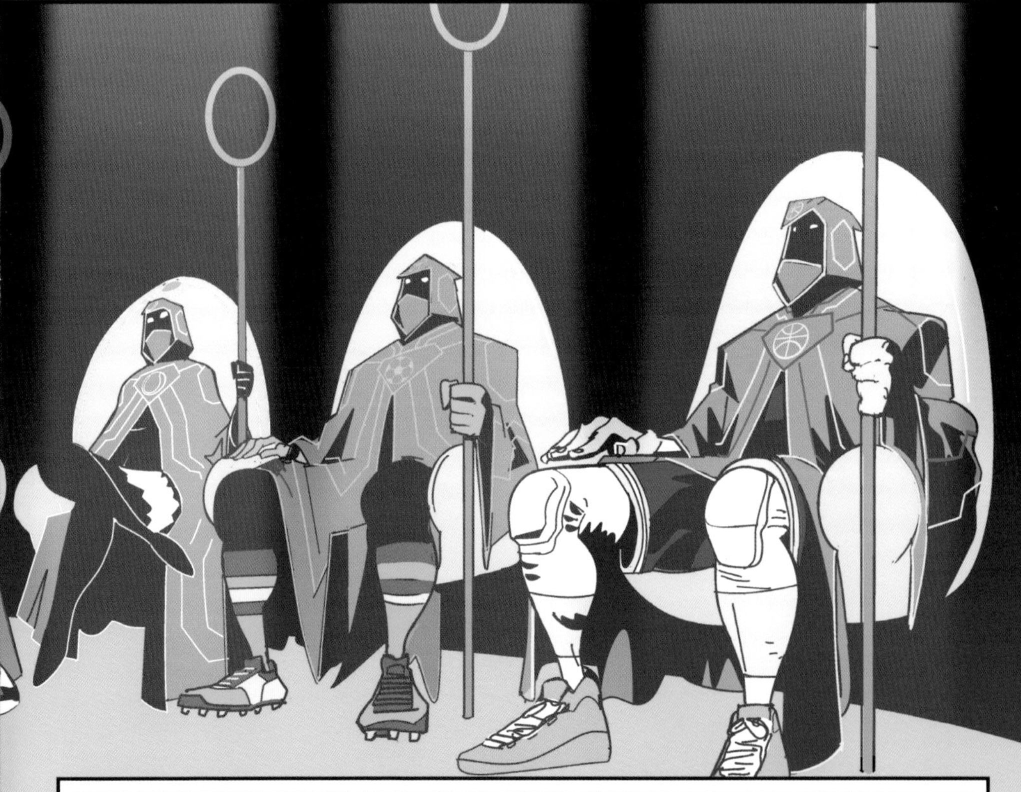

WHAT HAPPENS NEX-

YOU TWO WERE ABOUT TO MISS ALL THE ACTION!
YEAH, THESE SEATS ARE SO CLOSE IT'S LIKE YOU CAN ALMOST TALK TO STEPHEN CURRY.
UH, YEP. TOTALLY.

STEPHEN CURRY DRIBBLES UP THE RIGHT SIDE, WEAVING THROUGH DEFENDERS. CURRY CROSSES OVER, RISES UP FROM THIRTY FEET, AND
BANG!
HE NAILS A THREE-POINTER!
WINK
YEAAAH!

SIX MONTHS LATER.
BROOKLYN, NEW YORK.
DMG!
We need you again. It's time to find the next new sports superhero.
YOU'VE GOT TO BE KIDDING ME. NOW?
YES, NOW.
We're in the middle of a game.
NOT ANYMORE, YOU'RE NOT.

ALL RIGHT, THAT IS STILL PRETTY COOL! I LOVE THOSE OLD SPORTS SUPERHEROES!
DING!
Walk through the door.
Walk through the door.
What door?
Look again.

SHOOM
COME ON, JESSE, GUESS WE GOTTA FIND **SOMEONE ELSE** TO HELP SAVE SPORTS AND, WHO KNOWS, MAYBE EVEN THE **WORLD...**

YES WE DO, MY FRIEND. AND IF YOU THINK ABOUT IT, THAT KINDA MAKES ***US*** SUPERHEROES!
BUMP!

I STILL SAY THIS ***WHOLE THING*** IS ***WEIRD.***

TO BE CONTINUED...